John R. Angstadt U.S.M.C.

CHINA HORSE MARINE

AMERICAN LEGATION, PEIPING, CHINA 1934–1937

**I would like to dedicate this book to my uncle,
Private Matthew M. Mannherz**
Company "B" Marine Detachment
American Embassy, Peiping, China.
1936-1938

John R. Angstadt U.S.M.C.

CHINA HORSE MARINE

AMERICAN LEGATION, PEIPING, CHINA 1934–1937

E. RICHARD BONHAM

4880 Lower Valley Road • Atglen, PA 19310

Printed in The United States
ISBN: 978-0-7643-4890-7

We are interested in hearing from authors with book ideas on related topics.

Published by Schiffer Publishing Ltd.
4880 Lower Valley Road
Atglen, PA 19310
Phone: (610) 593-1777
FAX: (610) 593-2002
E-mail: Info@schifferbooks.com.

Visit our web site at: www.schifferbooks.com
Please write for a free catalog.
This book may be purchased from the publisher.
Try your bookstore first.

CONTENTS

FOREWORD

by Lt. Col. Michael Manifor U.S.M.C.

For more than forty years, U.S. Marines guarded American lives and property while serving as American Legation Guards in Peiping, China. These "China Marines" stood ready to protect when trouble threatened. They performed their duties with many comforts and few hardships. However, as they still do today in far off lands, they accomplished their job in the traditional manner of Sea Soldiers. Watching aggression come closer by the year, they maintained their tact and bearing in defending American interests.

It is widely known that none of the Marine Legation Guards were finer than the Mounted Detachment, the "Horse Marines." Membership meant you had the upmost in pride, bearing and military efficiency. One not only had to be a good horseman, but had to qualify with rifle, machinegun, pistol, and sword from the saddle. Only the best were chosen to ride the Mongolian ponies and gallop among the dust of the mounted. The Mounted Detachment knew better than anyone the surrounding country and the challenges of keeping track of every American in a bustling city.

Over the ages since their departure in 1941, the Legation Guard Marines have slowly faded and very few remain alive today. This wonderful book gives us a snapshot in time of the best of the China Marines. It shows us their daily routines… the drill, the sports, and the way these men bought their time in an enchanting and alluring environment filled with a "thousand-and-one" oddities. These until -now unpublished photos capture the scenes associated with the Mounted Detachment and their life in "Magic China": parades, dress uniforms and equipment; Chinese coolies, rickshaws, and businesses on the streets; and exquisite temples, shrines, and architecture of the Orient. The items and photos exhibited in this reference finely capture one Marine's memories of friends and adventure in a far off, mystical land.

As a Marine, a historian, and collector of Marine Corps militaria, I am delighted to know that the items belonging to US Marine Private John Angstadt, Embassy Legation Guard, Mounted Detachment, Peiping, China, can be shared in a manner befitting one of the Few and the Proud. The efforts of the author have ensured that these fine China Marines and their memories will live forever in the following pages.

Semper Fidelis,
LtCol Mike Manifor, USMC

BIOGRAPHY

of John W. Thomason Jr.

John William Thomason Jr., was born February 28, 1893, in Huntsville, Texas. Thomason attended Southwestern University, Sam Houston Normal Institute, The University of Texas, and the Art Students League in New York. He started his career as a writer and illustrator for the *Houston Cronicle* at the beginning of World War I.

In April 1917, Thomason was appointed a second lieutenant in the United States Marine Corps. While serving with the 49th Company, First Battalion, 5th Regiment (Marines), 2nd Division, AEF, Thomason fought in five major engagements and fourteen battles. During the Battle of Soissons, he was awarded both the Navy Cross and the Silver Star for gallantry in action.

During the war, he would draw whatever he saw around him, and those drawings became the basis for his most popular book *Fix Bayonets*, published in 1926. After the war, Thomason served in Cuba, Nicaragua, China, and on the USS *Rochester*. While stationed at the American Legation in Peiping, China, Thomason produced most of the drawings reproduced in this book. John Thomason was both a prolific and popular artist and author, having written and illustrated more than sixty stories for such magazines as *American Mercury*, *Scribner's* and the *Saturday Evening Post*. Thomason wrote and illustrated eleven books. Many of the period's most famous authors were close friends, including Ernest Hemmingway. During World War II, Thomason served in the Office of Naval Intelligence and on the staff of Fleet Adm. Chester W. Nimitz.

Thomason was promoted to Colonel in 1942 and died at San Diego Naval Hospital March 12, 1944. When the train bearing his body crossed into the state of Texas at El Paso, all official flags in Texas were lowered to half-mast in his honor. Many consider John W. Thomason the Poet Laureate of the United States Marine Corps.

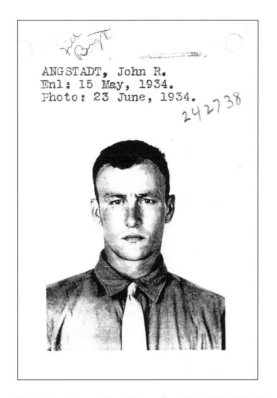

ANGSTADT, John R.
Enl: 15 May, 1934.
Photo: 23 June, 1934.
242738

BIOGRAPHY
of John R. Angstadt

John R. Angstadt was born May 30, 1912, in Steelton, Pennsylvania. He was the son of Cora Martin Blaine and John Angstadt. After graduating from Elizabethtown High School, Elizabethtown, Pennsylvania, in 1931, he enlisted in the United States Marine Corps on May 15, 1934, in Baltimore, Maryland.

After boot camp at Parris Island, South Carolina, he was assigned to the American Legation, Peiping, China. Angstadt left Norfolk, Virginia, on the USS *Chaumont*, sailing on September 25, 1934, and arriving at Chinwangtao, China, on December 9, 1934. On his arrival at the Legation, he was assigned to Company "B" Marine Detachment. Angstadt was later assigned to the Headquarters Detachment, Mounted Detachment on May 16, 1935. Angstadt served the remainder of his time in China with the Mounted Detachment. Angstadt was a member of the Post Tennis Team and played in the Peiping Chronicle Tennis League.

One of the duties of the Mounted Detachment was as the Legation Military Police. Angstadt was reassigned to Marine Detachment, Detention Prison, Receiving Station, Naval Operating Base, Norfolk, Virginia, and sailed from Chinwangtao, China, on the USS *Henderson* October 28, 1937. Angstadt was honorably discharged from the United States Marine Corps as a corporal on January 27, 1941. Angstadt later worked for the Office of Inspector General and retired in 1966. He died on August 14, 1989.

INTRODUCTION

My uncle was a China Marine. I grew up listening to my Uncle Matt's wonderful stories about his service in China during the 1930s. The tales were filled with the people, foods, and strange smells of an exotic country that a boy would remember so well. My uncle lied about his age when he enlisted in the Marine Corps and was only seventeen when he was sent to serve at the American Legation in Peiping, China. At that time, China could be compared to the American Wild West right after the Civil War: populated with bandits, thieves, and soldiers of fortune from all over the world. Matthew's stories featured many of these people, but he was most impressed with the small group of Horse Marines stationed at the American Legation, who patrolled the narrow streets of Peiping and the surrounding countryside on horseback.

The Horse Marines' job was to protect American missionaries and businessmen from the many bands of bandits roving the Chinese countryside. Each District was patrolled weekly, and a census was taken of American citizens residing in and around Peiping. The Mounted Detachment was considered the elite of China Marines. Another thing that influenced my interest in the China Marines was my discovery of the books and art of John W. Thomason. Thomason was a Marine officer who was also an artist and the author of many short stories written about his experiences serving in China during the 1930s. I was hooked.

Many years later, I was offered the Marine uniform and a group of Horse Marine items (by Major Mike Manifor, U.S.M.C.) that belonged to John R. Angstadt, who served with the Mounted Detachment at the American Legation in Peiping during the time of my Uncle Matt's service in China. Along with the group was a large photo album that documented Angstadt's service in China. The Angstadt collection is the basis for this book. This book is not a history of the Mounted Detachment, but rather, a history of Angstadt's service as a Horse Marine in China. I have been fortunate to receive permission from the Newton Gresham Library at Sam Houston State University to include many drawings done by John W. Thomason during his service in China to help portray what both Angstadt and my uncle observed during that time period. Also included are a few items from the Marine Corps Museum and from private collections to fill gaps in the Angstadt group. Most of the captions were written by Angstadt in his photo album. Throughout this book, I have tried to tell the story of John R. Angstadt and the Mounted Detachment with only period objects and photographs.

E. Richard Bonham
March 2014

ACKNOWLEDGMENTS

This book would not have been possible without the generous assistance I have received from the following people: Sam Bidleman, who photographed the John R. Angstadt group of objects and put the book into a workable form; Lt. Col. Mike Manifor, who kept the collection intact, answered my questions, and provided photographs from his collection; Felicia Williamson, Head, Thomason Special Collections, Sam Houston State University, Newton Gresham Library, who helped me include the drawings of John W. Thomason in this book; Owen L. Conner, Curator, Uniforms & Heraldry, National Museum of the Marine Corps; Alfred Houde, Supervisory, Curator (Ordnance), National Museum of the Marine Corps, for providing photographs of objects in the National Museum of the Marine Corps collection; Judy Labbe and Lisa Oaks from James Julia, Inc., who provided photographs from their catalogs; Kevin Hoffman, George Pradarits, and Lee Wolf, who gave me objects from their collections to photograph for this book; Bob Biondi and Ian Robertson from Schiffer Publishing, who graciously answered all of my dumb questions; Hank Truslow for his encouragement; Jack Laidacker for inspiration; and my wife Kathy Hummel, for her help and dealing with extra work taking care of our four dogs and cat.

Drawing by John W. Thomason
Thomason Special Collections, Newton Gresham Library, Sam Houston State University

Drawing by John W. Thomason
Thomason Special Collections, Newton Gresham Library, Sam Houston State University

American Embassy Guard Peiping, China

CHAPTER 1:
THE JOHN R. ANGSTADT GROUPING

Photograph by Sam Bidleman

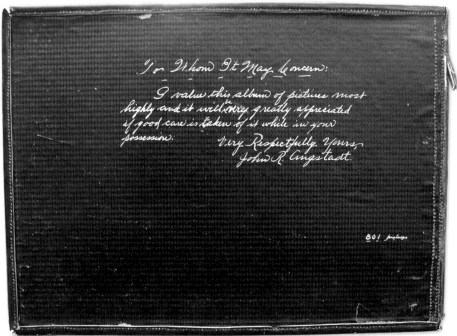

John R. Angstadt's photo album cover front and reverse.
Photograph by Sam Bidleman

Drawing by John W. Thomason
Thomason Special Collections, Newton Gresham Library, Sam Houston State University

John R. Angstadt and "Good Chance."

Chapter 1: The John R. Angstadt Grouping

John R. Angstadt's Marine Corps Marksmanship Qualification Badges

Angstadt earned the Marine Corps Marksman badge with clasps for Pistol-Dismounted, Rifle, Sword, and Bayonet. He also earned the Pistol Sharpshooter badge. Several of the photographs show that Angstadt also earned the Expert Rifleman badge with three clasps.

John R. Angstadt's Marine Corps Good Conduct Medal

The Marine Corps Good Conduct Medal was established by the Secretary of the Navy in July 1896. The medal recognizes good behavior and faithful service in the Marine Corps. Qualifying service consists of uninterrupted service with no convictions by court-martial, not more than one non-judicial punishment, and no lost time due to sickness misconduct or injury misconduct.

Photographs by Sam Bidleman

Pvt. John R. Angstadt with "Telegraph," Peiping, China, 1937.

Uniform reverse.

John R. Angstadt's "Blues" uniform and hat worn during his service as a member of the Mounted Detachment at the American Legation, Peiping, China, in 1937.

John R. Angstadt U.S.M.C., Horse Marine

Pattern 1925 "droop wing" EGA collar insignia.

Uniform with EGA collar devices worn by
Marines, 1926-1937.

J.R. Angstadt's name in the sleeve.

Note the grommets in the collar for the EGAs.

Large uniform coat button.

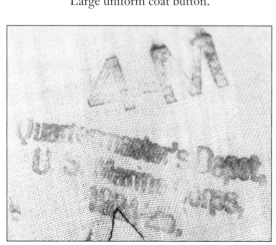

Quartermaster Depot. US Marine Corps, 1924-
1925. *Photographs by Sam Bidleman*

18

Uniform cuff and button.

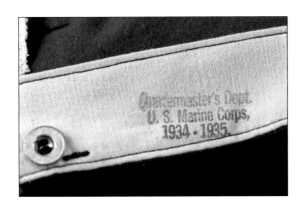

Angstadt's friends in Pomachang, China, 1936.

John R. Angstadt's "Blues" uniform trousers worn in China, 1934-1937. *Photographs by Sam Bidleman*

John R. Angstadt's Chinese silk-embroidered rememberance scroll showing
his service in Peiping, China, 1934–1937 (22 inches wide by 33 inches tall).
Made meticulously by local artists, these scrolls were a popular souvenir of Marines
and sailors that served in China. The same skilled artistry is depicted on the
cover of Angstadt's photo album. *Photograph by Sam Bidleman*

Details of Angstadt's silk scroll. *Photograph by Sam Bidleman*

Chinese-made Mounted Detachment patch
(Front) 7⅜" total height by 6¼" total width.

Chinese-made Mounted Detachment patch
(Back) 7⅜" total height by 6¼" total width.

Angstadt's Mounted Detachment's EGA Diamond fur hat.
Yellow enamel was used specifically by the mounted detachment.
Photography by Sam Bidleman

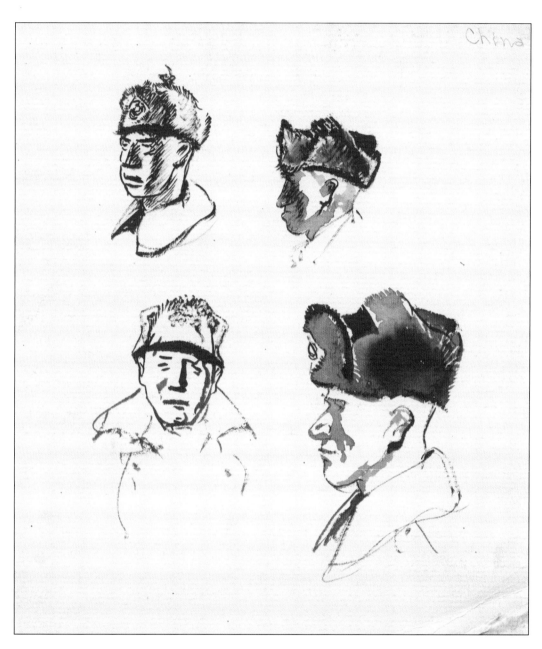

Drawing by John W. Thomason
Thomason Special Collections, Newton Gresham Library, Sam Houston State University

John R. Angstadt U.S.M.C., Horse Marine

This Mounted Detachment officer's fur hat was worn by Col. Bill Lee USMC while stationed at the American Legation, Peiping, China. *National Museum of the Marine Corps*

Yellow enameled Mounted Detachment officer's diamond. (*Michael Manifor Collection*)

White enameled Headquarters Company diamond. *National Museum of the Marine Corps*

Fur hat worn by the Headquarters Company at the American Legation, Peiping, China. *National Museum of the Marine Corps*

This hat was worn by John R. Angstadt while serving as a member of the Mounted
Detachment at the American Legation, Peiping, China, 1934–1937.
Photographs by Sam Bidleman

D. Pomerleau on duty.
Summer uniform.

Capt. James E. Webb's summer service hat (1937).
National Museum of the Marine Corps

Bowers on afternoon patrol.
Winter uniform.

Maj. Gen. Smedley Butler's winter service hat. Butler commanded the
Marine Expeditionary Force in China from 1927-1929. *National
Museum of the Marine Corps*

Chinese-Made Silver Cup
Marine-Army Rifle Match,
September 8th and 9th, 1931,
Peiping, China. First place was
won by 1st Sgt. Huff with a
score of 528. Height 5".
Photographs by Sam Bidleman

**John R. Angstadt's
Chinese-made
silver trophy cup**
*Photographs by
Sam Bidleman*

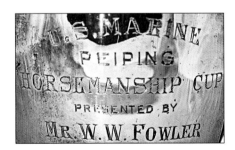

US Marine Peiping Horsemanship Cup
Presented by Mr. W.W. Fowler to
John R. Angstadt on "Good Chance"
20 April 1937

Pvt. J.R. Angstadt, winner of the Fowler Cup
American Embassy Guard News
Peiping, China, May 1937
Michael Manifor Collection

John R. Angstadt mounted on "Good Chance."

A group of Mounted Detachment Marines displaying their riding crops.

GUARD NEWS   JULY 1ST, 1936

Dust From The Mounted

The dust has cleared and the sound and fury abated enough to permit a man to safely record the results of the local turf classic known throughout North China as the Legation Guard's Cup Race, which takes place during the Spring Race Meeting at Paomachang. The field this year was composed entirely of horses from the stable of the Mounted Detachment of the American Embassy Guard. The race, a nine furlong affair, was won by "Vesper Belle", Pomerleau up, by two lengths. Second place went to "Whisky Bill", Bowers up, and third place to "Play Boy", Keplinger up. "Tipon", who is condsidered solely a steeplechase specialist, made a good showing in the flat race, getting a close fourth with Foster up. "Thunderbolt" remained true to form and took Ohran through the gate to the stables. He must be getting old as he usually jumps the rail.

Article from the
American Embassy Guard News

Russell A. Bowers

Pvt. Bowers' Chinese-made trophy riding crop, engraved "Peiping China," "Mounted Det.," "Whisky Bill," and "R. A. Bowers."
Crop on right/above is 34 ½" in total length.

"Winon," "Shannon," and "Baldy" with Pvt. Dwyer D. Burnett.
Note the Domed EGA roundel and two flat roundels

Eagle roundel on "Leatherneck."

Chrome-plated horse bit and eagle roundels
brought back from China by John R. Angstadt.

Photographs by Sam Bidleman

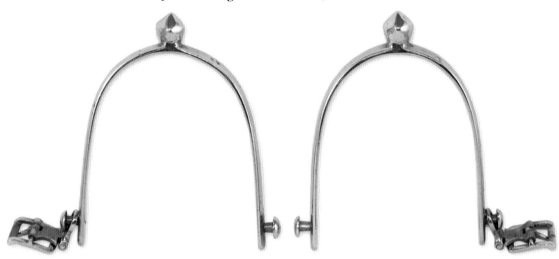

Angstadt's chrome or nickel-plated spurs.

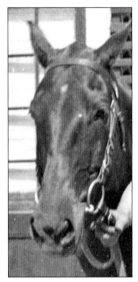

All metal horse tack and sword
hilts were plated for full dress.

The same spurs being worn
on Angstadt's riding boots.

Chrome-plated
watering bit.

Photographs by Sam Bidleman

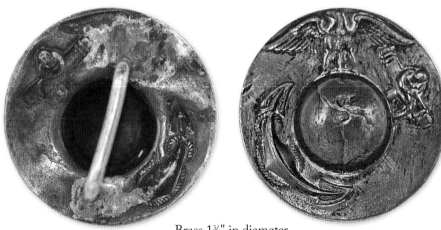

Brass 1¾" in diameter.
Photographs by Sam Bidleman

EGA rosette for a Mounted Detachment bridle brought back from China
by John R. Angstadt shown in the photograph with "Braun."

Angstadt's flag with Philadelphia Quartermaster Depot marking.
This may be a mounted used flag. Size 3" x 6".
Photographs by Sam Bidleman

CHAPTER 2:

THE MOUNTED
DETACHMENT IN 1934

THE MOUNTED DETACHMENT IN 1934

By Private Ralph H. Brooks.

he Mounted Detachment, which is the first organized cavalry unit in the Marine Corps, was organized in February, 1912, for the protection of American citizens. This organization took place shortly after the Revolution of 1911, but it was not until later that it was made a unit of the American Legation Guard. First Lieutenant David M. Randall was its first commanding officer.

Many changes have taken place since the Mounted was first organized. It originally consisted of 16 men; one sergeant, three corporals and twelve privates. Since that time it has grown to its present strength of one officer, two sergeants, one corporal, five pfcs. and twenty-three privates. Our present Troop Commander is Lieutenant Charles E. Shepard, Jr., who relieved Lieutenant Lewis B. Puller. Sergeant Harles L. Wilkinson is our Troop Sergeant, Sergeant Weisner F. Thomas is Stable Sergeant and Pfc. Gail L. Shoemaker is Veterinarian.

Among the various duties that the Mounted Detachment performs, besides our general routine of drills, inspections and parades, is the taking of the census of American citizens residing in and around Peiping. The city is divided into four districts, each squad of the Mounted being assigned a district to cover. The districts are patrolled weekly for the purpose of observing any change of address that may not have been reported. Once a year the concentration points are visited for the purpose of inspection and renewal of the flares that are used as distress signals as well as that of giving instruction in their use. The City Patrol was taken over by the Mounted Detachment on Labor Day of 1933. So far we have done quite well with it, and will continue to do so in the future.

170

The Detachment is armed with one machine gun, three Browning automatic rifles, three Sub-Thompson machine guns and twenty rifles. Every man is also armed with a .45 Colt automatic and a cavalry saber. The only men who do not carry rifles are members of the machine gun crew.

The Troop suffered a great loss this spring when the Countess de Martell left to join her husband in Syria. She has time and again given us some of our finest mounts, one of which was "Volnay." This pony has won the Guard Race on three occasions, and looks like a sure winner again. The Troop has three races a year; two flat races of a mile and a quarter, and either a steeplechase or a paper hunt. It is needless to say that there is a lot of argument as to who has the fastest pony and the races usually end with a "dark horse" nosing out the favorite. In the last flat race, "Volnay," with Stickles up, won easily by ten lengths, followed by "Vesper Belle," Tart up and "Chief," Gagner up. The first three places of every Guard Race are presented with cups and prize money, so one can see why the boys really work hard for a place.

We are equipped with the best veterinary facilities in North China. Sgt. Thomas and Pfc. Shoemaker are both very capable veterinarians and are fit to cope with any illness of animals which might arise. Our shoeing is done by a Chinese blacksmith and is inspected by the Stable Watch on duty.

The present stables were built in the summer of 1933 by men the of the Mounted. It was a lot of work, but we were proud of them after they were finished—although we did growl some at the time. It made things a lot more comfortable for the ponies, and after all, they do a lot for us and never complain and we all feel that they are deserving of a little of our time if it will make things better for them. Our barracks have just had a new coat of paint and a new floor which helps its appearance 100%, and we intend to keep it looking as good as it does at present.

171

1934 *American Embassy Guard Annual.*

It may be of interest to know that the McClellan saddles used by the Troop and the U.S. Cavalry are of the same type that were used in the Civil War. A blanket roll consisting of a complete change of clothes, including shoes and a blanket, can be secured to the cantel of the saddle, as well as saddle bags in which toilet articles and mess gear are carried in the near side, and grooming gear, feed and horseshoes in the off side. In addition to that a saber is attached to the saddle on the off side and a rifle boot on the near side. That is no doubt the reason that the U.S. Cavalry has never adopted another for its use, for it would be hard to find another saddle that would be as practical as the McClellan.

Although they are small in size, they can cover a surprising amount of ground in one day and be ready and fit to go the next we must give a lot of credit to these little Mongolian ponies that we ride. Their weight runs from about 650 pounds to about 725 pounds, and they average thirteen hands in height. They are usually in their prime at about six or seven years of age. The average jump for them is about three and a half feet. Because of the size of these ponies, men picked for the Mounted must weigh from 140 to 170 pounds. Each man coming to the Troop must have a clean record or he will not be accepted, and this is one of the reasons that we have one of the finest outfits in the Marine Corps.

At this writing we have not run the Pistol and Saber Course for record. For the past week we have been in training, and by the looks of the riding and the handling of the saber, we will have another 100% qualification. Although twenty men in the Troop have never run the Pistol and Saber Course, we are confidant that we will have a high average of qualification as these men are taking to the work like ducks take to water. It is not every man in the Marine Corps that has an opportunity to run this course, and of course every man does his utmost to get as much out of it as possible. Pharmacist Mate Second Class

172

Bond, who accompanies us on our cross-country rides and manoeuvers, also runs this course. Last year Bond showed some good riding and form by qualifying with both the pistol and saber, and we look for him to repeat this year. Following is the qualification for the Pistol and Saber Course;

Pistol. (Once over the course)
Expert   13 hits
Sharpshooter   10 hits
Marksman   8 hits
Time limit 55 seconds.

One less hit for every second over time.

One less hit for every time a horse breaks out of a gallop.

Saber (Twice over the course)
Expert Swordsman   90 percent
Excellent   85 percent
Swordsman   75 percent

Three points will be scored for piercing the dummy with the point of the saber. Two points may be scored for vigor of attack: that is, the spirit and fighting manner in which the lunges are made. If the vigor of attack is excellent, two points will be scored. If it is very good, one and one-half points and if it is fair, one point will be scored. Nothing will be scored for the vigor of attack if it is considered less than fair.

There are ten dummies in the course, and the possible score is 50, making the total possible score 100. For each second over the prescribed time limit of forty-five seconds, two points will be deducted from the total. For each obstacle not jumped, five points will be deducted from the score. For each instance during the run that the horse assumes a gait other than a gallop, one point will be deducted. This penalty will not be construed as applicable in the case of run-outs, or where the horse in changing leads hits two or more beats of a trot, or in refusals.

And so we close the 1934 training year, and in so doing we wish all our friends success and happy landings.

173

1934 American Embassy Guard Annual.

THE MOUNTED DETACHMENT IN 1935

By Private Gerald C. Merchant, Jr.

This detachment of "Horse Marines" happens to be the only authorized mounted detachment connected with the Marine Corps at the present time.

It was the first cavalry detachment in the Marine Corps, being organized in Feburary, 1912, as a result of the Revolution of 1911 for the protection of American citizens in the city of Peiping and vicinity. However, it was not until a later date that it was made a regular unit of the American Legation Guard.

The embryo of the Mounted Detachment consisted of sixteen men; one sergeant, three corporals, and twelve privates. Since that time, the complement has grown to a strength of thirty-one men; one sergeant, two corporals; the remainder being privates first class and privates. Until the middle of this year, an officer was in charge, but since then, the troop has been very ably handled by Sergeant Harles L. Wilkinson, who has been with the troop for quite a number of years. The record of the troop speaks for his effiency.

The duties of this Detachment, other than the regular drills and inspections, conforming to the rules and regulations of the U.S. Army Cavalry, are varied. The principal one is the compiling of a census of the American citizens residing in Peiping and vicinity. This census is taken anually. A very simple and uncomplicated system is used in this respect. The city is divided into four districts, each district containing on an average an equal number of citizens, and the men in the troop are divided accordingly, groups being assigned to each district, and these individual groups, each one with its leader, are responsible for their respective

113

1935 American Embassy Guard Annual.

districts. The census is compiled in the late fall, but once a week during the entire year, the districts are patrolled, in order that changes of addresses, etc., may be recorded.

Another duty performed by the Detachment is that of Military Police. To date, there has been no room for criticism in this respect, and we are sure that it will continue to remain so.

This Detachment, at present, is armed with eight Browning Automatic Rifles; in addition, every trooper has a forty-five Colt's automatic pistol, and a saber, (U.S. Army Cavalry). Then of course, there is the regular service rifle carried by every man in the Marine Corps.

McClellan saddles are standard equipment. They have been used by the U.S. Cavalry since the Civil War. On these saddles can be secured everything needed, such as clothing, toilet articles, blankets, etc., by the trooper on travels covering considerable distance and time. This saddle probably will remain in use by the cavalry for some time to come, as it would be next to impossible for another to be found as practical as this one.

Just prior to this writing, the Troop completed the Mounted Saber and Pistol course. It is with the greatest of pleasure that I am able to state that the record just made by this Detachment, in this respect, is one of the best ever attained as yet. The qualifications were as follows, Saber—Expert Swordsman—Fifteen men; Excellent Swordsman—Three men; and Qualified Swordsman—Five men. All men who ran this course qualified. The Pistol course resulted in a like good record, there being thirteen men making Pistol Expert—Mounted; eight men as Pistol Sharpshooter—Mount-

114

ed; and three as Pistol Marksman—Mounted. Also, all of the men running this course were qualified. We are very proud of this record and only hope that the troop will be able to keep such a record in the future. It may be of interest to know that this course is run in accordance to the rules of the U.S. Army Cavalry.

In the winter, when all of the crops of the country-side have been cleared, the troop indulges in cross-country rides once a week. It is during these rides that real riding ability is shown. They are not the least bit gentle and it is "every man for himself". There are slides, ditches, and many other obstacles, differing in nature, to overcome, and, also, many spills are to be witnessed. Riding cross-stirrups, off and on at a gallop, etc., are some of the methods of trick riding practiced. A lot of fun is had, and each winter the troop looks foward to these "cross-countries".

The veterinary accomodations of this Detachment are among the best in North China. All ailments of the ponies can be ably handled with the facilities at hand. Since the departure of Sergeant Thomas, our former veterinarian and stable sergeant, these duties have been performed by Private First Class Blackwood and Private Smith, supervised by Sergeant Wilkinson. It was with great sorrow and regret that the troop lost the services of Sergeant Thomas, who recently returned to the States. We wish him all of the luck in the world in his future undertakings.

A word about the little Mongolian ponies that are used by the Mounted. They average around six hundred fifty to seven hundred fifty pounds in weight, and about thirteen hands in height. They have an almost unbelievable amount of endurance, and are

115

1935 American Embassy Guard Annual.

very fast for their size. Most of the ponies are donated to the troop by different persons residing in Peiping or Tientsin who no longer desire to keep them but wish to give them a good home, and know that by sending them to the Mounted Detachment, they will have such a home. All of the ponies have their little idiosyncrasies, but with a little practice riding one can soon get used to them.

Then, there are the races, paper-hunts, etc., participated in by this Detachment during the year. There are several of these competitions and they are enthusiastically indulged in by members of the Troop. In the International Guard Races, the Mounted Detachment always emerges the winners.

During the parades and inspections of the American Embassy Guard, the Mounted Detachment, almost invariably, has the best line in the review, and this goes to show how well the Detachment is drilled in this respect. Good drill is very essential to any cavalry unit.

All in all, the diversified duties of the Mounted Detachment are not bad, and it is the desire of almost every-one in the Marine Corps to become a member of such an organization, and we, of the Mounted, consider it an honor to be a member of this Detachment. Only the best men of the Post are selected for this duty, and the records of the Detachment substantuate this fact. And so with this, we close the year of 1935.

116

1935 American Embassy Guard Annual.

Drawing by John W. Thomason
Thomason Special Collections, Newton Gresham Library, Sam Houston State University

Drawing by John W. Thomason
Thomason Special Collections, Newton Gresham Library, Sam Houston State University

CHAPTER 3:
THE MARINE MOUNTED DETACHMENT WEAPONS

"The Marine Mounted Detachment is armed with one machine gun, three Browning automatic rifles, three Sub-Thompson machine guns, and twenty rifles. Every man is also armed with a .45 Colt automatic and a cavalry saber." (*American Legation Guard Annual*, Peiping, China, 1934)

The Colt M1911 .45-caliber automatic pistol was the standard Marine Corps sidearm. This sidearm was carried by every member of the Mounted Detachment serving in China.

Target practice with the Colt M1911 in Haiti, 1926.

John R. Angstadt U.S.M.C., Horse Marine

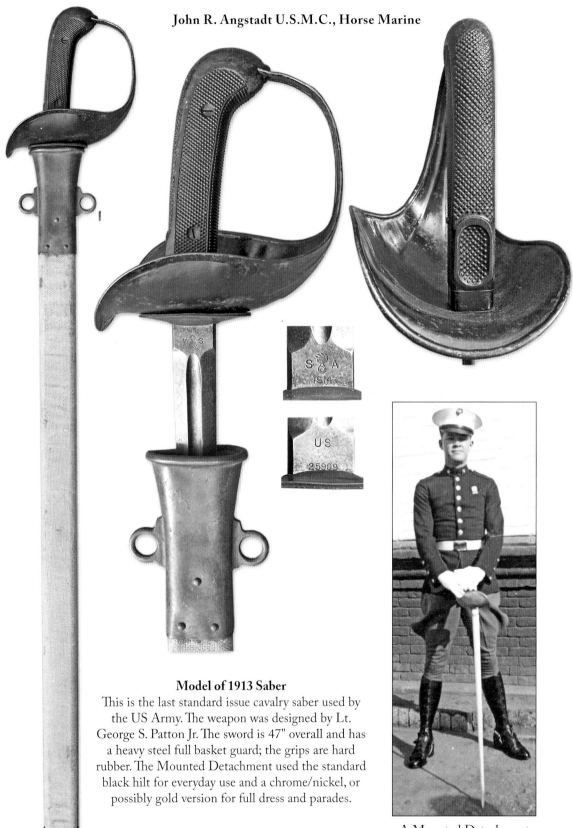

Model of 1913 Saber
This is the last standard issue cavalry saber used by the US Army. The weapon was designed by Lt. George S. Patton Jr. The sword is 47" overall and has a heavy steel full basket guard; the grips are hard rubber. The Mounted Detachment used the standard black hilt for everyday use and a chrome/nickel, or possibly gold version for full dress and parades.

A Mounted Detachment Marine in dress Blues with "Patton" saber.

Chapter 3: The Marine Mounted Detachment Weapons

China Marine in Shanghai (1937) with a M1928 Thompson submachine gun.

Colt M1921/28 Thompson submachine gun with vertical foregrip and a 50-round drum magazine. *James Julia Auctions*

M1928 Thompson submachine gun with a horizontal foregrip and a twenty-round detachable box magazine.

The Marine Corps purchased 621 Colt Thompson submachine guns between 1926 and 1928. The Thompson proved very popular with Marines fighting in Nicaragua, Haiti, South America, and China. The Thompsons were used with both vertical and horizontal foregrips. Twenty-round box magazines and fifty-round drums were also used.

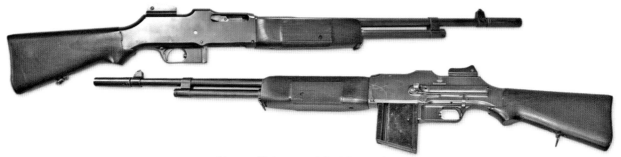

National Museum of the Marine Corps

M1918 Browning automatic rifle chambered for the .30 M1906
cartridge with a 20-round detachable box magazine.
National Museum of the Marine Corps

National Museum of the Marine Corps

A Mounted Detachment
Marine with a Browning
Automatic Rifle and a
Colt M1911, Chinadega,
Nicaragua, 1928. The
Marine to his left has an
M1903 Springfield rifle.

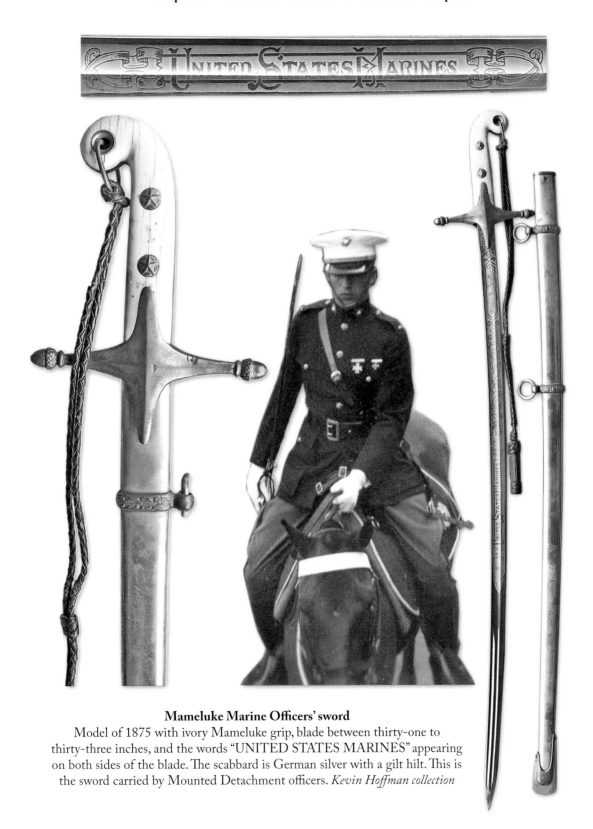

Mameluke Marine Officers' sword
Model of 1875 with ivory Mameluke grip, blade between thirty-one to
thirty-three inches, and the words "UNITED STATES MARINES" appearing
on both sides of the blade. The scabbard is German silver with a gilt hilt. This is
the sword carried by Mounted Detachment officers. *Kevin Hoffman collection*

John R. Angstadt U.S.M.C., Horse Marine

US Magazine Rifle, Caliber .30, 1903
The M1903 Springfield was the standard US service rifle at the time of Angstadt's service in China. The rifle weighs 8.7 lbs. and fires the 30-06 cartridge from a 24" barrel. The rifle was carried in a leather scabbard on the saddle by all members of the Marine Mounted Detachment. The humpback handguard was designed to protect the rear sight when the rifle was thrust into a cavalryman's rifle scabbard.

Rowland W. Randall with a M1903 Springfield.

M-1917 helmet as worn by the Mounted Detachment, American Legation,
Peiping, China. The front of the helmets are painted with a diamond.

John R. Angstadt U.S.M.C., Horse Marine

Drawing by John W. Thomason
Thomason Special Collections, Newton Gresham Library, Sam Houston State University

American Embassy Guard Peiping, China

CHAPTER 4:
THE MARINE MOUNTED DETACHMENT ON PARADE

Battalion Commanders Color Guard, Mass Formation, and the Mounted.

The Mounted Detachment in a Column of Sections.

Chapter 4: The Marine Mounted Detachment on Parade

Headquarters, Mounted Detachment flag.

Passing in review, eyes right.

Passing in review.

The Band.

Daily parade: A – Johnson Hall; B – Ice Rink.

The Staff.

At the gallop.

A column of sections.

The pride of the Embassy: the Mounted Detachment.

Waiting in line for the Adjutant's call.

The Salute.

John R. Angstadt U.S.M.C., Horse Marine

Circa 1935 Marine Officer "Montana Peak" Campaign or Field Hat. Officer hats were prescribed red and gold cords. The EGA is of the 1914 Pattern, but was worn through the 1930s. (*Michael Manifor Collection*)

At the Gate.

Mounted Detachment colors.

John R. Angstadt U.S.M.C., Horse Marine

The All Arms Trophy.

Receiving the "All Arms Trophy" for the best looking outfit, 1935.

The gang in blues.

Ready for inspection.

John R. Angstadt U.S.M.C., Horse Marine

Drawing by John W. Thomason
Thomason Special Collections, Newton Gresham Library, Sam Houston State University

American Embassy Guard Peiping, China

CHAPTER 5:
MEMBERS OF THE MOUNTED DETACHMENT

"Brawn" and Angstadt.

"Blue Streak" and C. B. Jones.

"Bantam" and Spoltore.

"Telegram" and Greenland.

"Quid" and Garrett.

"Tarboy" and Burns.

"Whiskey Bill" and Hays.

"Flare" and Wilson.

"Anchors Aweigh" and Asher.

"Sunny Boy" and McAlpin.

"Telegram" and Greenland Blues.

"Sea Gull" and Swaicki.

"Can Do" and Spiering.

"Baijon" and Baker.

"Baldy" and Harisin.

"Vesper Belle" and Donald D. Pomerleau.

"Can Do" and Burnett.

John R. Angstadt U.S.M.C., Horse Marine

Technical Sergeant George J. Nowack, Headquarters Detachment, Marine Mounted Detachment, American Embassy, Peiping, China. Technical Sergeant Nowack served in the Marine Corps Expeditionary Force, Culebra, Puerto Rico, Headquarters Company, Eleventh Regiment, Ocotal, Nicaragua, Headquarters Company, First Brigade, United States Marine Corps, Port Au Prince, Republic Of Haiti, and twice with Headquarters Detachment, Marine Mounted Detachment, American Embassy, Peiping, China, as a Veterinarian. He is pictured here with his mount "Shannon" at the American Embassy, Peiping, China, in 1936.

"Ace O' Hearts" and Julius F. Fliszar.

"Telegram" and Yeager.

"Blue Streak" and Gaw (the Bat).

"Baldy" and Clyde D. Therrien.

"Reveille" and Jerry W. Zachidny.

"Tin Hat" and Larry P. Chiara.

"Za Za" and Allien.

"Tipon" and George Hreha.

"Winon" and Burnett Sturdivan.

"Leatherneck" and Lasch.

"Pluto" and Mearz.

Fox on "Cymbal."

The long and the short of the Mounted: Marsh and Spoltore.

Angstadt on "Telegraph" off side.

Angstadt on "Telegraph" near side.

Our Gang with Sully and Trooper.

Members of the Mounted Detachment displaying their swords. Note the Navy Corpsman assigned to ride with the Mounted Detachment standing in the center of the group.

American Embassy Guard Peiping, China

CHAPTER 6:
SADDLES OF THE
MOUNTED DETACHMENT

McClellan saddles are standard equipment for the Mounted Detachment and are the
same type used by the US Cavalry. An M1913 Patton saber is attached to the off side and a
rifle boot containing an M1903 Springfield Rifle is attached to the near side.

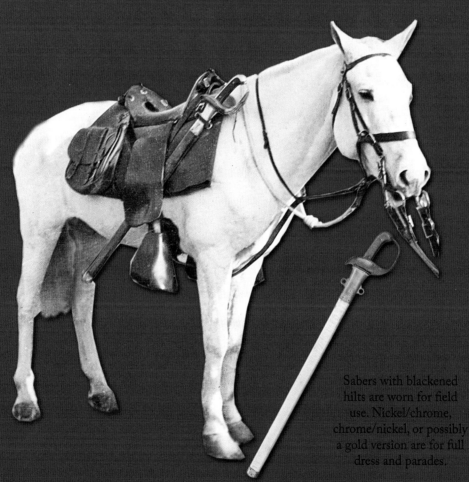

Sabers with blackened
hilts are worn for field
use. Nickel/chrome,
chrome/nickel, or possibly
a gold version are for full
dress and parades.

John R. Angstadt U.S.M.C., Horse Marine

"Telegram" and Greenland.

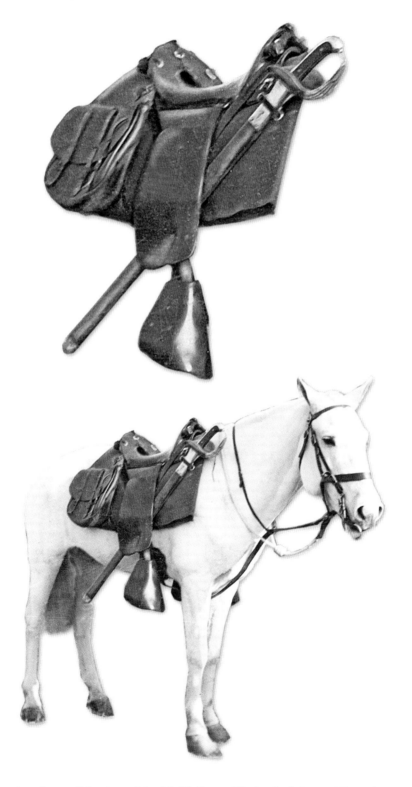

Detail showing the modification of the McClellan saddle by the Mounted Detachment.
A long leather skirt has been added to protect the uniform trousers from the saddle's straps.
Also note the attachment of the M1913 Patton saber to the McClellan saddle.

John R. Angstadt U.S.M.C., Horse Marine

Drawing by John W. Thomason
Thomason Special Collections, Newton Gresham Library, Sam Houston State University

American Embassy Guard Peiping, China

CHAPTER 7:
THE WILLIAM B. HALE FUNERAL

William B. Hale (22), a member of the Mounted Detachment, took his own life by a self-inflicted gunshot wound on July 5, 1937. William Hale enlisted in the United States Marines in January 1935, and had been stationed at the American Legation, Peiping, China, for the previous year and a half. Franklin O. Hale (20), a younger brother who was also in the Marine Corps and a member of the Mounted Detachment, was stationed in Peiping for several months with his brother.

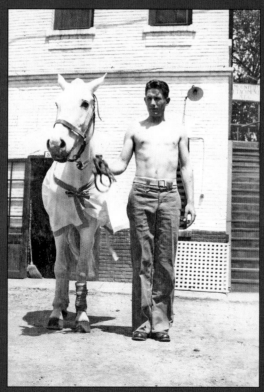

William B. Hale with "Telegram," Deceased.

The Escort.

W.B. Hale's mount "Telegram" with Baker.

Bearing the Corps.

The Pallbearers.

Final Rites.

Young Hale and Officers.

Chapter 7: The William B. Hale Funeral

The Corps.

The Service.

The Procession.

Rendering Honors.

Colors at Half Mast.

Corporal of the Japanese Guard. Peking 1932

This is a more refined type that average. I tried to get a more typical soldier to pose, but Col. Aihara, the commandant personally selected this fellow and I had to take him.

Drawing by John W. Thomason
Thomason Special Collections, Newton Gresham Library, Sam Houston State University

American Embassy Guard Peiping, China

CHAPTER 8:
THE SECOND SINO-JAPANESE WAR

The 1937 Sino-Japanese War was the result of the Empire of Japan's desire to dominate China both militarily and politically, to secure China's vast reserves of raw materials, food, and labor. Japan invaded Manchuria in 1931 and created the Japanese puppet state of Manchukuo. The Japanese had also provoked several "incidents" to expand Japan's control of China. On the night of July 7, 1937, Japanese and Chinese troops exchanged fire in the vicinity of the Marco Polo Bridge, which was a crucial access route to Peiping. The initial skirmish soon escalated into a full-scale battle and marked the beginning of total war between the two countries. Marines were just spectators to all the aggression, and the Peking Legation's demise was in 1941, when the Marines, without the means to resist, were ordered to surrender.

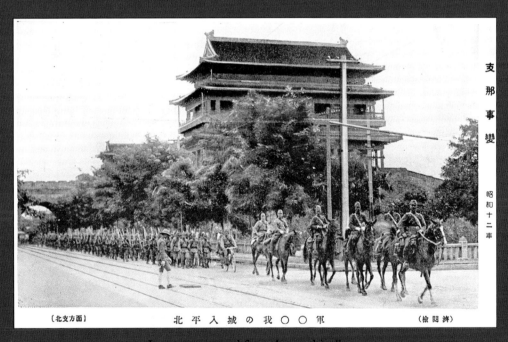

支那事變

昭和十二年

〔北支方面〕　　北平入城の我〇〇軍　　（檢閱済）

Japanese postcard from Angstadt's album.

Chinese sentry.

Chinese soldier guarding the Peiping city wall.

Japanese troops entering Tankuantum city.

Japanese troops entering Peiping.

Japanese artillery in Peiping.

Japanese postcard from Angstadt's album.

Drawing by John W. Thomason
Thomason Special Collections, Newton Gresham Library, Sam Houston State University

John R. Angstadt U.S.M.C., Horse Marine

支
那
事
變

昭
和
十
二
年

〔北支方面〕　　　　前線視察の同邊部隊長　　　　（檢閲済）

Japanese postcard from Angstadt's album.

Chinese General Shang Chang commanding the 37th Chinese Army.

124

Dead Chinese soldiers, Tientsin, China.

Japanese trenches outside Tientsin, China.

Fighting in the hills west of Peiping.

Japanese warplane.

Drawing by John W. Thomason
Thomason Special Collections, Newton Gresham Library, Sam Houston State University

Drawing by John W. Thomason
Thomason Special Collections, Newton Gresham Library, Sam Houston State University

CHAPTER 9:
SPORTS

Sports were a very important part of life to John R. Angstadt and all of the Marines stationed at the American Legation in Peiping during the 1930s. The Marines competed among themselves in Inter-Company matches at the Legation and with other American Marines and Army and Navy personnel stationed around China. There were also many international sports competitions between Marines and the members of the various foreign Legation Guards stationed in Peiping. About the only sport not played at the Legation was American football. Angstadt's game was tennis; he was part of the Legation Tennis Team and played in the Peiping Chronicle Tennis League.

Angstadt warming up, spring 1937.

Legation Tennis Team; they played in the Peiping Chronicle Tennis League.
Angstadt is second from right, bottom row.

Inter-Company tug-o-war.

International Tug-O-War, Italians versus Marines.

Pole vault at the intra-company track meet.

International Guard's Meet Tug-O-War medal for second prize, won by F.J. Murphy, 1935.
National Museum of the Marine Corps

Ice hockey at Yenching University.

International track and field meet.

Inter-company Tug-O-War.

CHAPTER 10:
DOGS OF THE
MOUNTED DETACHMENT

Trooper and Sully.

John R. Angstadt U.S.M.C., Horse Marine

Cantonese, Hong jao 1932

Drawing by John W. Thomason
Thomason Special Collections, Newton Gresham Library, Sam Houston State University

American Embassy Guard Peiping, China

CHAPTER 10:
DOGS OF THE
MOUNTED DETACHMENT

Trooper and Sully.

Sergeant Trooper with a Chinese medal.

Sully and Bully.

Lee and Sully.

Trooper on top of the Horseshoer building.

Drawing by John W. Thomason
Thomason Special Collections, Newton Gresham Library, Sam Houston State University

CHAPTER 11:
THE AMERICAN LEGATION AND PEIPING, 1934–1937

John R. Angstadt and the other members of the Mounted Detachment spent most of their time at the American Legation and patrolling the countryside around Peiping. The Mounted Detachment was responsible for compiling an annual census of American citizens residing in and around Peiping. The Mounted were also responsible for the protection of those American citizens. Another duty performed by the Detachment was that of Military Police. Marines did a lot of "tourism" to such popular sites as the Tartar Wall, Forbidden City, Ming Tombs, and the Great Wall.

The firing line at Peiping, China.

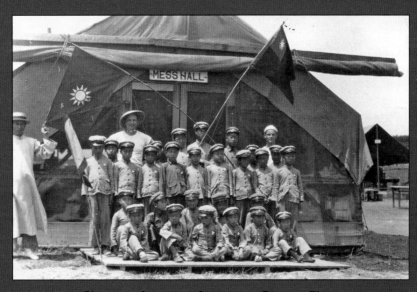

Chinese cadets at our firing range, Peiping, China.

Out for a winter ride in Peiping.

The Pagoda in winter.

Nine Dragon Screen, Peiping.

Chien Men from the Tartar Wall.

Jones at the Forbidden City.

Burns at the Winter Palace.

The ramp of the Tartar Wall.

Number two military gate, Peiping.

Hataman Street in Peiping, showing part of a funeral.

At the Temple of Heaven, Peiping.

Marine watching a camel train near Peiping.

Angstadt and Braun on the Tartar Wall.

Tar Boy and Jones at the Princess Tomb.

C. B. Jones on a marble horse at the Princess Tomb.

Mannherz and rickshaw.

Matthew celebrating on the athletic field.

British and American Marines.

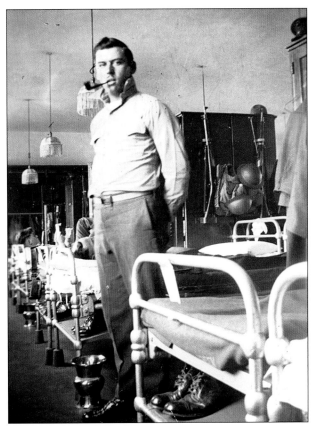

The Barracks.

Our Barracks and athletic field.

Home of the Mounted and my bicycle.

Selling water from a water wheel barrow, Peiping.

American Drug Store, Peiping.

Debner in Peiping.

Bowers going up the Great Wall in a chair.

A camel train at the Great Wall.

Bowers on the Great Wall.

CHAPTER 12:
SOCIAL LIFE OF
THE MOUNTED

The exchange rate of the US dollar in comparison to the Mexican silver dollar—the standard currency in pre-World War II China—was very high. Because of the high exchange rate, even Marine privates lived very comfortable lifestyles. Inexpensive goods, clothing, and cheap labor were readily available, and Marine squads were able to hire Chinese houseboys to do all of their cleaning, mending, and washing. Because China Marines had money to spend and a great deal of free time, their social life was very active. Marines sought attention and dates from the young Russian ladies of the Legation. Many Russians were there after being displaced by the Russian Civil War in the 1920s and were essentially stateless.

Baldy, Angstadt, and Valia.

Pomereau, Zenia, and Vesper Belle.

Lily and Valia.

Bomb heaven and Italian marines on the Tartar Wall.

Valia and Angstadt at Pei Hai.

Valia with Shishi in the Forbidden City.

Valia

John R. Angstadt U.S.M.C., Horse Marine

John R. Angstadt U.S.M.C., Horse Marine

Drawing by John W. Thomason
Thomason Special Collections, Newton Gresham Library, Sam Houston State University

American Embassy Guard Peiping, China

CHAPTER 13:
OFFICERS OF THE MOUNTED DETACHMENT

Col. Presley M. Rixey Jr.,
Commanding Officer of the American Legation.

John R. Angstadt U.S.M.C., Horse Marine

Drawing by John W. Thomason
Thomason Special Collections, Newton Gresham Library, Sam Houston State University

American Embassy Guard Peiping, China

CHAPTER 13:
OFFICERS OF THE
MOUNTED DETACHMENT

Col. Presley M. Rixey Jr.,
Commanding Officer of the American Legation.

John R. Angstadt U.S.M.C., Horse Marine

Drawing by John W. Thomason
Thomason Special Collections, Newton Gresham Library, Sam Houston State University

American Embassy Guard Peiping, China

CHAPTER 13:
OFFICERS OF THE MOUNTED DETACHMENT

Col. Presley M. Rixey Jr.,
Commanding Officer of the American Legation.

John R. Angstadt U.S.M.C., Horse Marine

Drawing by John W. Thomason
Thomason Special Collections, Newton Gresham Library, Sam Houston State University

American Embassy Guard Peiping, China

CHAPTER 13:
OFFICERS OF THE MOUNTED DETACHMENT

Col. Presley M. Rixey Jr.,
Commanding Officer of the American Legation.

John R. Angstadt U.S.M.C., Horse Marine

Col. Presley M. Rixey Jr.

Lt. Frederick A. Ramsey Jr. "Fearless"
Commander of the Mounted Detachment.

Capt. Bird.

Capt. Robert B. Lucky.

Lt. Col. James, "Telegram," and Jeager.

Drawing by John W. Thomason
Thomason Special Collections, Newton Gresham Library, Sam Houston State University

American Embassy Guard Peiping, China

CHAPTER 14:
THE AMERICAN EMBASSY GUARD ANNUAL & NEWS

The *American Embassy Guard Annual* and the *American Embassy Guard News* were published by and for the personnel of the Marine Guard at the American Embassy, Peiping, China. John R. Angstadt brought home his Annuals for the years 1934 and 1935. Each annual gives a history of the American Embassy at Peiping, China, and the activities of each Company, Detachment, and department of the Marine Guard. A photograph of every member of the Marine Guard was also published. The 1934 Annual included portraits of each member of the Mounted Detachment, along with their horses; all of these portraits are included in this chapter. The *American Embassy Guard News* was a monthly magazine publishing news of the legation for that month. Advertisements for local businesses were also included in each publication.

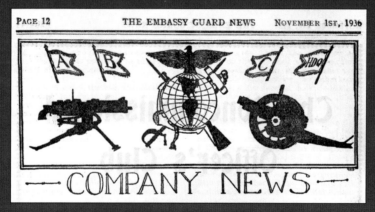

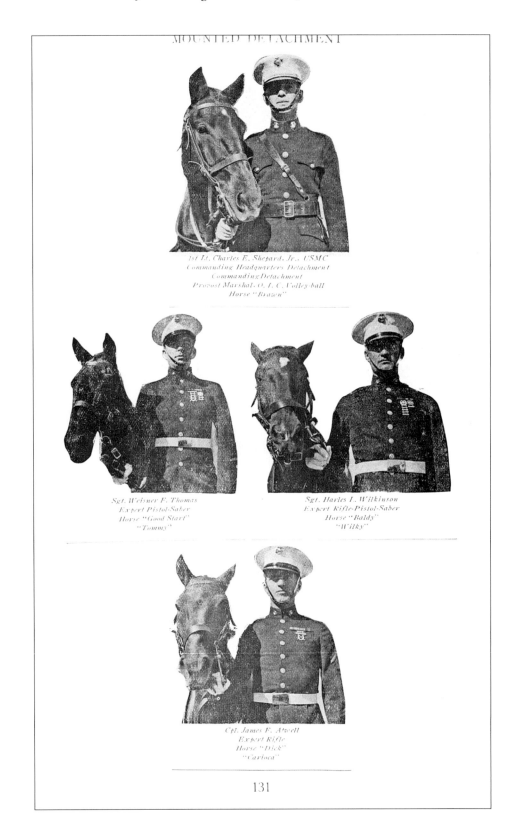

MOUNTED DETACHMENT

1st Lt. Charles E. Shepard, Jr., USMC
Commanding Headquarters Detachment
Commanding Detachment
Provost Marshal, O. I. C. Volley-ball
Horse "Brazen"

Sgt. Weisner F. Thomas
Expert Pistol-Saber
Horse "Good Start"
"Tommy"

Sgt. Harles I. Wilkinson
Expert Rifle-Pistol-Saber
Horse "Baldy"
"Wilky"

Cpl. James F. Atwell
Expert Rifle
Horse "Dick"
"Carioca"

131

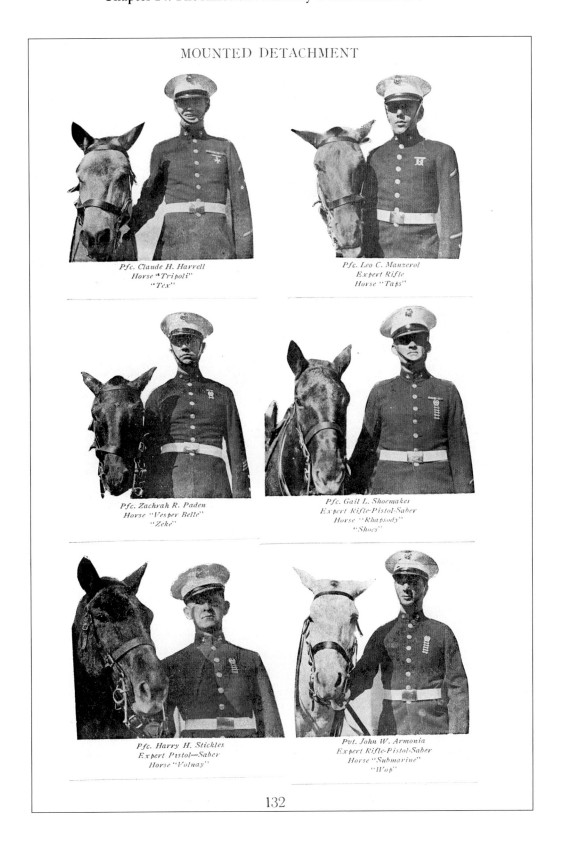

MOUNTED DETACHMENT

Pfc. Claude H. Harrell
Horse "Tripoli"
"Tex"

Pfc. Leo C. Manzerol
Expert Rifle
Horse "Taps"

Pfc. Zachrah R. Paden
Horse "Vesper Belle"
"Zeke"

Pfc. Gail L. Shoemaker
Expert Rifle-Pistol-Saber
Horse "Rhapsody"
"Shoes"

Pfc. Harry H. Stickles
Expert Pistol—Saber
Horse "Volnay"

Pvt. John W. Armonia
Expert Rifle-Pistol-Saber
Horse "Submarine"
"Wop"

132

MOUNTED DETACHMENT

Pvt. James B. Blackwood
Expert Pistol
Horse "Winon"
"Blackie"

Pvt. Ralph R. Brooks
Expert Pistol-Saber
Horse "Buck"
"Open House"

Pvt. Curtis W. Bush
Horse "Can Do"
"Bad Hop"

Pvt. Armand A. Chauvin
Horse "Sir Falstaff"
"Frenchy"

Pvt. Harry W. Clough
Horse "Tipon"

Pvt. James W. Dawson
Expert Pistol
Horse "Blue Streak"
"Dicky Boy"

133

MOUNTED DETACHMENT

Pvt. John E. Duty
Horse "Pat"

Pvt. Frank M. Flynn
Expert Pistol
Horse "Berry"
"Micky"

Pvt. Russell S. Harper
Horse "Bill"

Pvt. Boyd D. Jackson
Horse "Skipper"
"Jack"

Pvt. Thomas W. Johnston
Horse "Syossett"
"Johnnie"

Pvt. Lewis E. Lake
Horse "Clown"
"Sister"

134

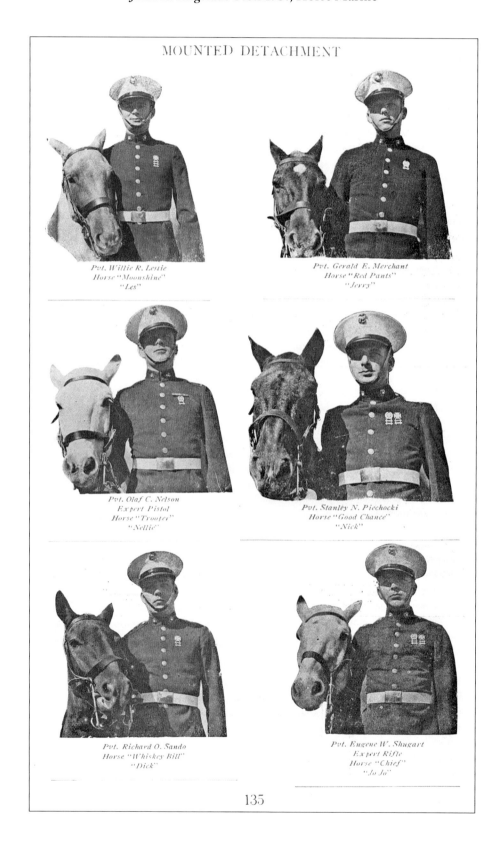

MOUNTED DETACHMENT

Pvt. Willie R. Leslie
Horse "Moonshine"
"Les"

Pvt. Gerald E. Merchant
Horse "Red Pants"
"Jerry"

Pvt. Olaf C. Nelson
Expert Pistol
Horse "Trooter"
"Nellie"

Pvt. Stanley N. Piechocki
Horse "Good Chance"
"Nick"

Pvt. Richard O. Sando
Horse "Whiskey Bill"
"Dick"

Pvt. Eugene W. Shugart
Expert Rifle
Horse "Chief"
"Jo Jo"

135

MOUNTED DETACHMENT

Pvt. Harry Smith
Expert Pistol-Saber
Horse "Playboy"
"Smitty"

Pvt. Ray S. Stowell
Horse "Nino"
"Chick"

Pvt. Allen F. Wilkinson
Horse "Tar Boy"
"Wilky"

Pvt. Oral V. Wilson
Horse "Sonny Boy"
"Willie"

136

John R. Angstadt U.S.M.C., Horse Marine

Dust From The Mounted

With this publication of the "Dust" we welcome into the Troop Privates Spoltore, McAlpin, Mays, Burns, Dille, Maerz, Allien and Bassett. These man are now active members in the Mounted Detachment of the American Embassy Guard—the only authorized mounted unit in the Marine Corps at the present time. Since its organization in February of 1912, when it was organized as a result of the Revolution of 1911, for the protection of American citizens in the city of Peiping, it has enjoyed and maintained a splendid reputation for being a unit of high military efficiency. The departure of each boat takes from us a portion of our personnel and to their replacements we say "*Carry On*". We hope that these new men shall enjoy their tour of duty with the Detachment, and that they shall make many fast friends. No doubt they shall.

We also welcome back to the Troop—Private Nick Yaeger, whom we lost to the Sick Bay for several days with ear trouble. We hope he has had the last of his illness.

We finally found out why it was that "Swampy" Marsh was seen leaving the office of the Peiping Chronicle. We understand that he wished to place the following in the "Lost and Found" column: *Lost—a horse. Color—black. Name—Thunderbolt. Lost in vicinity of Happy Valley.* Why not put a bell on him, Marsh?

How about three of our members who, after imbibing of sundry potions at the Privates' Club, obeyed that "prospecting urge" at the corner of Hataman and the Boulevard and started looking for gold with the able assistance of all of the available ricksha boys? We understand that the gold was in the shape of Brother Hays "Store" molars!

Out at the Rifle Range on the last cross-country ride who was it that let his mount, "Taps", roll without first removing the saddle? And men, 'Twas not only once, *but thrice*! I won't mention any names but I understand he's a pretty good vet.

And in cidently who is it that romps around the parade ground during parade with his saber at "high port"? Pssst. Psst. Gaw! Psst. "Carry Sabers!"

I hear that a good way to get in one's afternoon athletics is to ask Brother Spoltore what his new nickname is. I think it starts with S. A word of advice is to put on your track shoes before popping the question!

To top things off, in the midst of my painful search for copy in comes one of our luminaries and tells me that if he makes this issue of the "Dust" I get no more my evening "cup o' joe". Oh, woe is me! The things I endure for the press. And so, to bed.

K. W. G.

Cookcoos And Bakerbugs

Chief Cook Johnson came in the other morning with rouge and lipstick smeared all over his face. And he seems to be receiving quite a bit of local mail lately. Wonder just what is his secret of success? Also heard that he was starting a singing class in the near future.

The day after the last boat left we saw Mork holding sea-bag drill, but he decided to stay with us for a while longer. Could it be on account of the local girl-friend? She *is* good looking!

One of the Field Cooks seems to be the un-crowned King of the

PATRONIZE OUR ADVERTISERS

166

Page from the *American Embassy Guard News*, Peiping, China, July 1, 1936.

John R. Angstadt U.S.M.C., Horse Marine

"Jim"
The Mascot of the Mounted
Detachment.

The Mounted Breaks A Tough One
"Wild West Style"

Advertisements from the *American Embassy Guard Annual*, 1935.

JAPANESE LEGATION GUARD

Main barracks building

The Minister's Gate
Japanese Legation

A relic of the Boxer uprising
a captured Chinese gun

Headquarters,
Japanese Legation Guard

Lt. Col. M. Hasegawa,
Commandant,
Japanese Legation
Guard

Military Gate,
Japanese Legation Guard

A machine gun section in action

Japanese soldiers at play

Changing guards; the old and new
guards at the Military Gate

Transportation section

63

Page from the 1935 *American Embassy Guard Annual.*

John R. Angstadt U.S.M.C., Horse Marine

BRITISH LEGATION GUARD

Lions and guns standing guard

A reminder of the Boxer uprising

Entrance to British Legation

Major Jebens, M.C., Commandant, British Legation Guard

Entrance to British Minister's quarters

On guard

The Sergeants' Mess

Officers' Club

Relaxation

Guard of the day

Page from the 1935 *American Embassy Guard Annual*.

FRENCH LEGATION GUARD

A relic of the early China Coast privateers; French Guard Compound

The French Minister's Gate

Colonial infantrymen in working uniform

MAJOR J. J. LEGRANDE
Commandant, French Legation Guard

Officers and men enjoying the Guard library

The Guard of the day

The 3rd company (European) of the 16th Regiment, French Colonial Infantry

Placque in memory of French soldiers killed during the French-British march on Peking in 186

The French Non-com's Mess

French Non-coms entertain Sgt. Cramer and Cpl. Thetford

65

Page from the 1935 *American Embassy Guard Annual*.

ITALIAN LEGATION GUARD

Main Entrance to Italian Legation

Mounting Guard

Shades of the bounding main; a
section of the sleeping quarters

Tenente di Vascello Gino
Spagone, Commandant,
Italian Legation Guard

The artillery unit in action

The Military Gate

Memorial to Italian dead
in Boxer uprising

Colors

Italian Guard schoolroom

The Commandant sampling
the food; a daily ritual

66

Page from the 1935 *American Embassy Guard Annual.*

CHAPTER 15:
SAILING TO CHINA AND RETURNING HOME

After boot camp at Parris Island, South Carolina, Angstadt was assigned to the American Legation, Peiping, China. Angstadt left Norfolk, Virginia, on the USS *Chaumont*, sailing on September 25, 1934, and arriving in Chinwangtao, China, on December 9, 1934. After his assignment with the Mounted Detachment, Angstadt was reassigned to Norfolk, Virginia, and sailed from Chinwangtao, China, on the USS *Henderson*, October 28, 1937.

EMBARKED ON BOARD U. S. S. CHAUMONT

At *Norfolk, Va* On *25 Sept. 34*

And sailed therefrom *28 Sept. 34*

Arrived at *Chinwangtao, China* On *9 Dec. 1934*

And disembarked *10 December, 1934*

J Monahan

Captain U.S.M.C.

USS Chaumont 4-11-34-3000

USS *Chaumont.*

Bob on USS *Chaumont*.

Radio room on USS *Chaumont*.

Debner on USS *Chaumont*.

USS *Chaumont.*

UNITED STATES SHIP HENDERSON

CHINWANGTAO, CHINA

Embarked on board U. S. S. HENDERSON at

on OCT 2 8 1937 , Sailed OCT 2 8 1937

Arrived *Mare Island Calif* Date DEC 16 1937

Disembarked DEC 16 1937

R. E. HILL,

First Lieutenant, U. S. M. C.

USS *Henderson. Courtesy Bureau of Construction and Repair, Navy Department*

John R. Angstadt U.S.M.C., Horse Marine

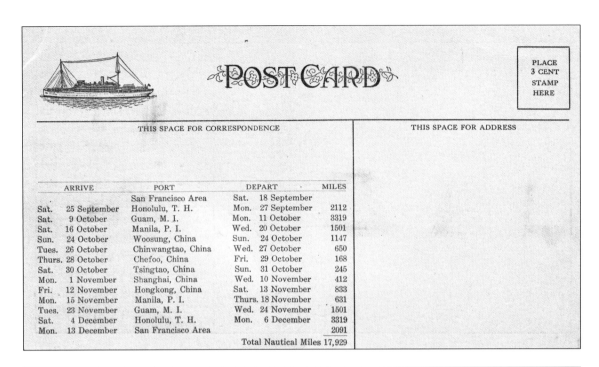

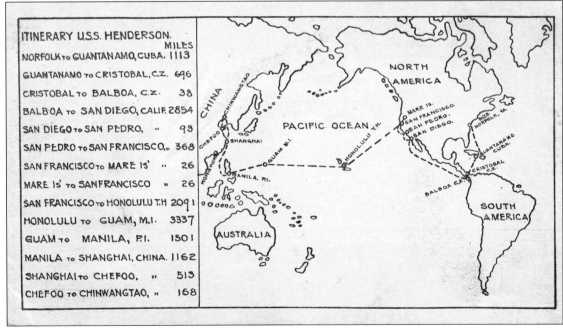

USS *Henderson* postcard.

The end of the
Typhoon. We ate
sandwiches and
coffee for three days.

A Freighter in Manila harbor.

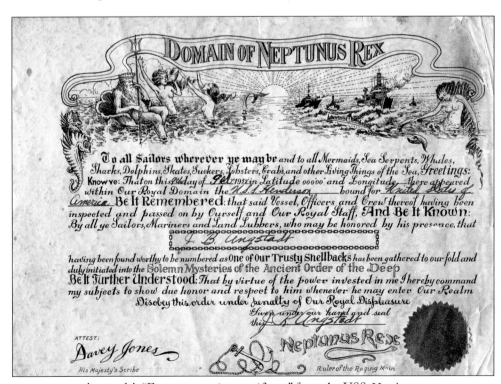

Angstadt's "Equator crossing certificate" from the USS *Henderson*.

John R. Angstadt U.S.M.C., Horse Marine

Drawing by John W. Thomason
Thomason Special Collections, Newton Gresham Library, Sam Houston State University

American Embassy Guard Peiping, China

CHAPTER 16:

THE MARINE MOUNTED DETACHMENT IN NICARAGUA

The following series of photographs document a Marine Mounted Detachment on patrol around Ocotal, Nicaragua, in September 1928. Ocotal was considered a hotbed of Nicaraguan rebel activity. This is one year after the Battle of Ocotal, which occurred in July 1927. A large force of rebels loyal to Augusto César Sandino attacked the garrison of Ocotal. The garrison was held by a small group of US Marines and Nicaraguan National Guard. The rebels were defeated with heavy losses thanks to a squadron of five DeHavilland DH-4 biplanes each armed with machine guns and four twenty-five pound bombs. The rebels suffered 156 killed and wounded, while the Marines and the National Guard suffered very light casualties. The Marines on the patrol are part of the 48th Company, 2nd Battalion, 5th Marine Regiment. The patrol is commanded by Lt. Sol Levensky, and he is accompanied by Capt. Hicks and Gunnery Sgt. John J. McKenna. These photographs are from Lt. Levensky's photograph album.
The picture captions are notes made by Lt. Levensky on the rear of the photographs

Before the jacks were put on and we were organizing, you see me rolling a cigarette.

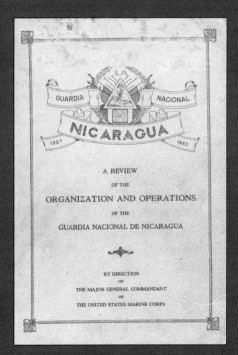

A review of the organization and operations of the Guardia Nacional de Nicaragua. This book documents the Marine Corps' involvement in Nicaragua from 1927-1933.

They are falling in to march off.

"There am I and my Grey Dick. Capt. Hicks and Gy. Sgt. McKenna are in the foreground."
(Note the EGAs on the corner of the officer's saddle blankets.)

Patrol mounted and ready to move out.

The lead of Hick's patrol starting from the Barrack's (sic).

"Just a few of my men along a typical road. It's mighty tough going on roads of this kind. The bottom is uncertain and the horse can almost swim. What a road?"

Just another view of myself and my men.

Capt. Hicks and Lt. Lewensky's patrol passing through the town of Ocotal, Nicaragua.

The well armed patrol, dismounted, near Ocotal.

FIRST BATTALION
Fifth Regiment, Second Brigade,
U. S. Marine Corps.

Managua,   Nicaragua.

THANKSGIVING
1930.

Second Nicaraguan Campaign Medal
Civil war broke out in Nicaragua in 1926, led by Gen. Augusto César Sandino, who rejected a negotiated agreement between the government of Nicaragua and the United States. Sandino led a sustained guerrilla war against the conservative regime and US Marines assigned to establish a neutral zone for the protection of American citizens. This medal was issued to members of the Marine Corps for service in Nicaragua between August 27, 1926, and January 2, 1933. *George Pradarits Collection*

This gun case is custom made for a Thompson submachine gun and was used by mounted Marines in Nicaragua. *Courtesy of the Lee Wolf collection*

Lieutenant Boyd, Ocotal, Nicaragua, 1929.

Lieutenant Boyd and two other Mounted Detachment officers, Ocotal, Nicaragua, 1929.

Marine Guardia pack train near Chipote, Nicaragua, 1927.

Mounted Detachment of the 77th Company, 2nd Battalion,
5th Marine Regiment, Ocotal, Nicaragua, 1927.

CHAPTER 17:
THE MARINE MOUNTED DETACHMENT IN HAITI

After a long period of civil strife, the United States military involvement in Haiti began on July 28, 1915, when US Marines and Naval forces invaded Port-au-Prince, Haiti, beginning two decades of US occupation. Between 1915 and 1934, Marine officers and enlisted men commanded and trained the Gendarmerie d'Haiti to protect United States citizens and interests. Marines went into the interior to subdue native Cacos, who were rebelling against the government by terrorizing people and disrupting transportation and communications. This occupation lasted until 1934.

The following photographs are from the photo album of Clarence E. Flook, who served as a Marine in the 36th Company, 2nd Regiment, First Brigade US Marine Corps, Port Au Prince, Haiti, 1925-1927.

(George Pradarits Collection)

The Haitian Campaign Medal, 1919-1920.

(George Pradarits Collection)

US Marine Mounted Detachment patrolling in the Haitian jungle, 1926.

Mounted Marine, Haiti, early 1930s.

Mounted Marine military policeman (MP) on patrol, Port Au Prince, Republic of Haiti, 1927.

Watering horses, Haiti, 1934.

Marine Mounted Detachment patrol, Haiti, 1927
(note the Browning automatic rifle across the saddle).

John R. Angstadt U.S.M.C., Horse Marine

Pvt. Clarence Flook and friend with Browning automatic rifles, Haiti, 1927.

The Presidents Guard, commanded by a Marine officer, Haiti, 1926.

Drawing by John W. Thomason
Thomason Special Collections, Newton Gresham Library, Sam Houston State University

Drawing by John W. Thomason
Thomason Special Collections, Newton Gresham Library, Sam Houston State University